W9-ASL-558

P·I·C·T·U·R·E·P·E·D·I·A

NOTE TO PARENTS

This book is part of PICTUREPEDIA, a completely
new kind of information series for children.
Its unique combination of pictures and words
encourages children to use their eyes to discover and
explore the world, while introducing them to a wealth
of basic knowledge. Clear, straightforward text
explains each picture thoroughly and provides
additional information about the topic.

"Looking it up" becomes an easy task with
PICTUREPEDIA, an ideal first reference for all types of
schoolwork. Because PICTUREPEDIA is also entertaining,
children will enjoy reading its words and looking
at its pictures over and over again. You can encourage
and stimulate further inquiry by helping your child
pose simple questions for the whole family to
"look up" and answer together.

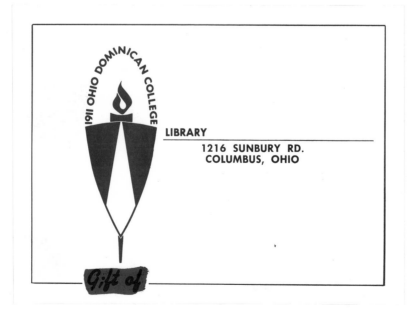

1911 OHIO DOMINICAN COLLEGE

LIBRARY
1216 SUNBURY RD.
COLUMBUS, OHIO

Gift of

J 500 Sci

Science

SEP 1999
RECEIVED
OHIO DOMINICAN
COLLEGE LIBRARY
COLUMBUS,

SCIENCE

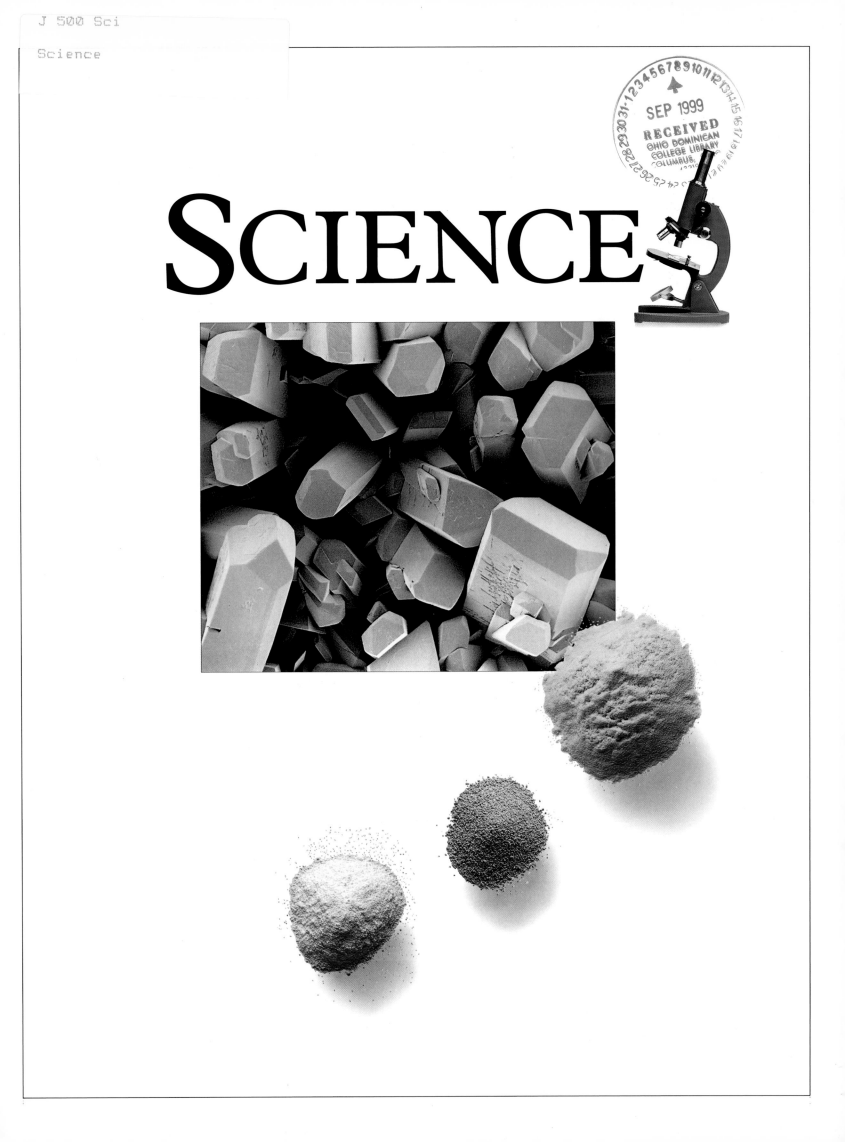

A DORLING KINDERSLEY BOOK
Conceived, edited, and designed by DK Direct Limited

Consultant Diana Maine

Project Editor Deborah Chancellor
Art Editor Ron Stobbart
Designer Tuong Nguyen

U.S. Editor B. Alison Weir

Series Editor Sarah Phillips
Series Art Editor Paul Wilkinson

Picture Researcher Paul Snelgrove

Production Manager Ian Paton

Editorial Director Jonathan Reed
Design Director Ed Day

First American edition, 1993
4 6 8 10 9 7 5 3
Published in the United States by
Dorling Kindersley, Inc., 232 Madison Avenue
New York, New York 10016

Copyright © 1993 Dorling Kindersley Limited, London

All rights reserved under International and Pan-American Copyright Conventions.
No part of this publication may be reproduced, stored in a retrieval system,
or transmitted in any form or by any means, electronic, mechanical, photocopying,
recording, or otherwise, without the prior written permission of the copyright owner.
Published in Great Britain by Dorling Kindersley Limited.
Distributed by Houghton Mifflin Company, Boston.

CIP data for this book is available.

Reproduced by Colourscan, Singapore
Printed and bound in Italy by Graphicom

SCIENCE

DK

DORLING KINDERSLEY
LONDON • NEW YORK • STUTTGART

CONTENTS

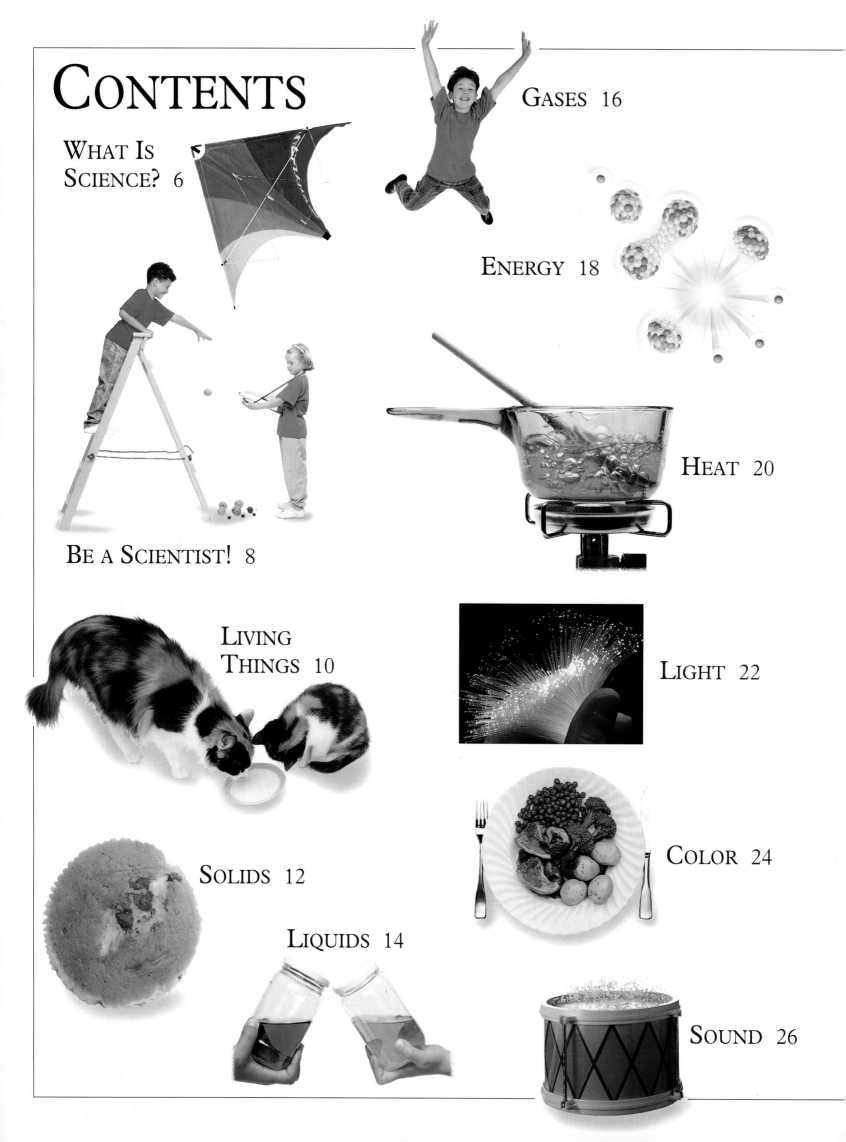

WHAT IS SCIENCE? 6

BE A SCIENTIST! 8

LIVING THINGS 10

SOLIDS 12

LIQUIDS 14

GASES 16

ENERGY 18

HEAT 20

LIGHT 22

COLOR 24

SOUND 26

FORCE AND MOVEMENT 28

MACHINES 30

ELECTRICITY 32

MAGNETS 34

WATER 36

WEATHER 38

MATERIALS 40

BALANCE OF NATURE 42

TIME 44

SCIENCE IN OUR LIVES 46

GLOSSARY & INDEX 48

WHAT IS SCIENCE?

You don't need to walk into a laboratory to see science in action. Science is all around you, every day of your life. Even at the most ordinary picnic, science is staring you in the face! There are three main kinds of science. The science of the natural world is called biology. Chemistry is the study of what things are made of and how they behave when they are mixed together. Physics looks at the rules of how things in the whole wide universe work.

Power stations can pollute the air. Biologists find out about the effects of pollution on nature.

Ice melts in the heat. Chemists study what makes changes like this happen.

Flying Physics
How does a kite fly in the sky? The force of air pushing upward underneath the kite is stronger than the pressure of air pushing down on it. The laws of flight are called aerodynamics and are studied in physics.

This ball is on the ground because an invisible force, called gravity, is pulling down on it. Physicists discover how different forces work.

The universe stretches out beyond the sky. Physicists study the distant planets.

We are living things! Biologists look at how our bodies work.

Living Biology

Like all living things, this dandelion makes copies of itself. In biology, this is called reproduction. The dandelion produces seeds, which are then carried away by the wind. The seeds then take root in the ground and grow into new plants.

Plants and animals are all part of the living world studied in biology.

Chemical Reaction!

A chemical reaction happens when you fry an egg. The runny, clear liquid of the raw egg turns white and hard when you cook it. In chemistry, chemical reactions change the way things look, feel, taste, and smell.

Radios are very complex machines. Physicists explain how different machines work.

A number of ingredients were mixed together to make this cake. Chemists look at what makes up different substances.

BE A SCIENTIST!

Scientists are full of curiosity. They never stop asking questions and trying to figure out the answers to them. They explore everything that exists, from the tiniest particle to the huge expanse of the universe. They ask how and why things happen as they do. Scientists are like detectives, always on the lookout for clues. Anyone can be a scientist! All you need to do is look around you. Ask a question, think up an idea for answering it, and then test your idea in a fair way.

Stargazer
Many scientists are fascinated by the universe. They use radio telescopes like this one to study the stars in space.

Does a big orange fall faster than a small grape?

Compare the sizes of the different pieces of fruit.

Hold on tight! Science experiments must always be carried out safely.

The things you use in a science experiment are called pieces of apparatus.

1. Watch Out!
Watching things carefully can make us ask questions about the world around us. If a bowl of fruit is knocked over by accident, does the big fruit hit the ground first?

2. Guess before You Test
Predicting, or guessing what will happen before you start, is an important part of an experiment. Before you begin, talk about the possible results with a friend.

3. Be Fair!
Make sure your experiment is fair by only testing one idea at a time. Each piece of fruit must be tested in exactly the same way.

Marvelous Medicine

Scientific discoveries can happen quite by chance. Early this century, a young scientist named Alexander Fleming found some specks of mold attacking some bacteria in a small dish. The mold was the base for penicillin, an antibiotic drug that we now use to fight infection and save lives.

Powerful microscopes help us see tiny bacteria. Penicillin kills this kind of bacteria.

Types of antibiotics

Fleming's bacteria dish

Scientists at Work

Scientists are ordinary people who sometimes work in very unusual places, all around the world. They may carry out experiments indoors in laboratories, or outdoors in many different weather conditions.

Each piece of fruit must be dropped from the same height.

Every measurement must be written down.

Use the same stopwatch to time each fall.

Ask Me Another . . .

Results can often lead to new questions and new experiments. If big and small things fall at the same speed, why does a feather fall more slowly than a pea? Tests show that the shape of an object affects how quickly it falls.

4. What Happened?

Science experiments often involve writing down results. The short time that each piece of fruit takes to fall must be carefully measured.

Check to see if your first guess was right.

All sizes of fruit can be tested.

5. Surprise Discovery

Your results may surprise you. Small fruit falls just as fast as big fruit. One strong force pulls them all down to the ground at the same speed. This force is called gravity.

LIVING THINGS

You are a living thing. All living things are made up of cells, and your body is made up of many billions of cells. Your cells join together to make tissues – for example, muscles. Tissues combine to make organs, like your heart. Biologists are scientists who study living things. They have divided the world of living things into groups, called kingdoms. The study of plants is called botany, and the study of animals is called zoology.

Cherries

Seaweed

Moss

Fly agaric fungus

Bacteria and Fungi Kingdoms
Bacteria are so tiny, they can't be seen without a microscope. They have a simple, one-cell structure. Bacteria and fungi feed on other living things and recycle the remains.

A kitten grows up into a cat. All living things grow.

Splitting Up
Living things are made up of at least one cell. For a living thing to reproduce and grow, its cells must keep on splitting into identical pairs. This single-cell bacterium divides every 20 minutes. Look how many bacteria there are after one hour.

Now

20 minutes later

40 minutes later

One hour later

All living things make copies of themselves. This is reproduction.

Living things all find some way of breathing. A cat breathes through its nose.

Living things need food to stay alive.

Plant Kingdom

There are many different kinds of plants. Some are soft and small enough to hold in your hand. Others are enormous and woody. Some plants have flowers, but others don't. Green plants use sunlight and water to make their own food.

Sweet chestnut

Poppy heads and seeds

All living things get rid of waste products.

Gerbera flower

Raft spinner

Hoverflies

Badger

Animal Kingdom

Animals have billions of very complex cells. Most of the world's animals, like insects, do not have backbones. Animals with backbones include mammals, birds, reptiles, amphibians, and fish.

Hen with chicks

Grass snake

Everything that lives, moves, but you can't always see the movement.

Lovely Lashes

Some people have tiny mites living in their eyelashes. The mites feed on liquid from the eye, cleaning the lashes at the same time. The mites need people, and people need them. Many living things depend on each other.

Spotted Salamander

A cat hears with its ears. Every living thing is sensitive in some way to the world around it.

Cuban hock

Shore crab

Rudd

11

SOLIDS

Everything is made up of matter. Molecules are the building blocks of matter. In solids, molecules are usually packed together in a regular way, so the solid keeps its shape without needing a container to hold it. Most matter is visible, like the pages of this book, but some is invisible, like air. Matter may be solid, liquid, or gaseous and change from one state to another.

Hydrogen atom

Uranium atom

Amazing Atoms

The smallest amount of a pure substance is called an atom. The simplest atom is hydrogen, but other atoms are more complex. Atoms are incredibly tiny – about 100 billion atoms fit on this period.

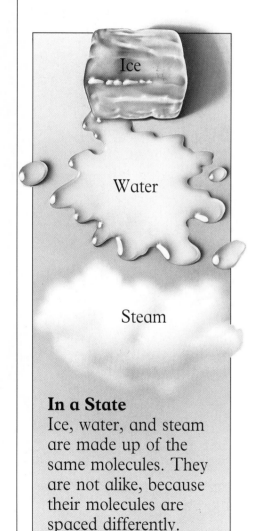

Ice

Water

Steam

Molecules in a Solid

Each of these children is acting the part of a molecule in a solid.

The children are all wearing red T-shirts to show that the molecules are all the same.

The molecules in most solids make up a very regular pattern.

In a State

Ice, water, and steam are made up of the same molecules. They are not alike, because their molecules are spaced differently. Solid ice melts into liquid water. When water is boiled, it turns into a gas, called steam.

Solids on Show

You can tell these solids apart because they do not look, feel, weigh, or smell the same. They all have different properties.

A flower is soft and delicate.

A muffin is crumbly and tasty.

Making Molecules

Atoms link up to make molecules. Two atoms of hydrogen join together to make one molecule of hydrogen gas.

The molecules in a cool solid do not move about very fast. If a solid is heated, the molecules move about faster and faster.

There are strong links between the molecules in a solid. This means that solids have a fixed shape.

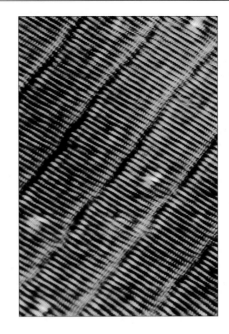

Larger than Life

These long, thin wax molecules are shown about 3 million times larger than they are in real life. The tiny blue dots are atoms that have joined together to make up the wax molecules.

Sugar

Crystal Clear

Grains of sugar are solid crystals. Their atoms are close together and arranged in a regular pattern, called a lattice. Many solids that look smooth actually have a crystalline structure, like these vitamin C tablets.

Vitamin C crystals, seen through a microscope

Vitamin C tablets

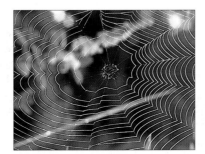

A shell is hard and brittle.

A spider's web is light and strong.

Graphite and Diamond

Graphite is soft and is used in pencils, and diamond is the hardest solid in the world. But diamond and graphite have a lot in common! They are two different forms of carbon. This means they have the same molecules, but they are arranged in different ways.

LIQUIDS

If you spread some butter on hot toast, the butter melts. When a solid gets hot enough to melt, it turns into a liquid. Liquids behave differently from solids. The heat that melts a solid breaks down some of the strong links between the molecules, so that the molecules can move about more freely. A liquid flows because its molecules can't hold together strongly enough to form a solid shape.

Syrup flows slowly.

Car oil flows quite well.

Ink flows very easily.

Sticky Spoonful
Some liquids flow much more easily than others. Liquids that are viscous do not flow well.

Molecules in a Liquid
These children are behaving like molecules in a liquid.

Fair Shares?
Who has more milk to drink? It may not look like it, but these glasses hold the same amount. Containers of different shapes can hold the same volume, or amount, of liquid.

Liquid Levels
Liquids flow to fill containers of any shape or size. The surface of a liquid always stays level, however much you may tilt the container.

Too Hot to Handle?

Ice cream melts easily, but not all solids have such low melting points. Some only melt if they are heated to very high temperatures. The steel in this factory melts at 2,700°F (1,500°C).

On the Boil

When a liquid is heated to a certain temperature, it turns into a gas. This temperature is called the boiling point. Different liquids have different boiling points. Water boils at 212°F (100°C).

In a liquid, the molecules are separate from each other.

Moving molecules can get right into all the corners of a container. This is why liquids take on the shape of the container that holds them.

Molecules in a liquid move about faster than molecules in a solid.

Molecules in a liquid are not arranged in a regular pattern, so they can move about freely.

On the Surface

Molecules near the surface of a liquid pull toward each other. A drop keeps its shape because of this surface tension. If some dish soap is added to a water drop, the surface tension is made weaker, so the drop spreads out.

Good Mixers

Cranberry juice mixes well with water. It dissolves completely.

Bad Mixers

Some liquids do not mix at all. Oil does not dissolve in water.

GASES

Gases are all around us and can't usually be seen or felt, but some can be smelled. All smells are molecules of gas mixed in the air. If you smell some tasty soup, you are actually sniffing in molecules of the soup. When you heat a liquid, it turns into a gas. The heat makes the molecules in the liquid move about faster and faster. The gas molecules fly off in all directions, spreading through the air.

Lighter than Air
When a gas gets hot, it takes up more room and gets lighter. A hot-air balloon rises up in the air because the air inside it is hot and much lighter than the air outside.

Molecules in a Gas
Each child is acting like a molecule in a gas. Look how they are bumping into each other.

There are no links between any of the molecules in a gas.

Dancing on Air
When a shaft of light shines through a gap in the trees, specks of dust look as if they are dancing in the sunlight. What is really happening is that the molecules in the air currents move about, flicking the dust in all directions.

As a gas spreads, the molecules get farther and farther apart. Gases will always spread to fit the space they are in.

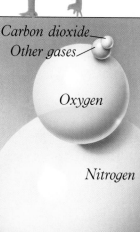

Carbon dioxide
Other gases
Oxygen
Nitrogen

In the Air
There are a number of different gases in the air we breathe. About 78 percent of air is nitrogen gas. Oxygen makes up 21 percent. Carbon dioxide and a variety of other gases make up just 1 percent of the gases in the air.

Pumping Air

It is easy to squash together, or compress, gas molecules. When you pump up a tire, you compress air molecules into a small space. The more air molecules you pump in, the more they push against the inside of the tire. The tire gets harder because pressure increases inside it.

High Pressure

Air presses on everything on Earth. You can see air pressure at work. If you suck juice out of a carton, the carton buckles. This is because air pressure pushing on the carton is greater than air pressure inside the carton.

Molecules in a gas move very quickly, darting about in all directions.

Night and Day

Plants help keep the balance of gases in the air. Night and day, they take in oxygen and "breathe out" carbon dioxide, as we do. But by day, they also take in large amounts of carbon dioxide, which they need to make their food, and give off oxygen.

Carbon dioxide

Carbon dioxide

Oxygen

Oxygen

Out of Breath

Gases can dissolve in liquids, and oxygen from the air dissolves in water. Fish need oxygen to breathe, so they use the oxygen in water to survive underwater. Humans also breathe oxygen, but unlike fish, we can't breathe underwater without a supply of compressed air.

ENERGY

Energy is needed for life and for every single movement in the whole universe. When you have run a race, you may feel that you have used up all your energy. But your energy has not been lost. It has changed into different kinds of energy: movement and heat. When work is done, energy is never lost, but it changes into other kinds of energy. Movement and heat energy are just two of the many different kinds of energy.

Jumping Jack
When the lid is closed, the puppet's spring is coiled up, ready to push the puppet out of the box. We say the spring has potential energy. When you open the lid, the spring's potential energy turns into movement energy.

Energy Changes
We can't make energy or destroy it. Instead, energy can change from one kind to another. This toy robot shows how energy may not stay in one form for very long!

Eating Energy
We get our energy from food, and we need to eat plants, or animals that have eaten plants, to stay alive. Plants get energy to grow from sunlight, so our energy really comes from the Sun.

Sun Power
Living things that grew millions of years ago were buried under rock, where they slowly turned into coal, oil, and gas. Energy from these fuels comes from the Sun, shining long ago.

1. When the robot is switched on, chemical energy stored in the batteries turns into electrical energy.

Batteries

2. As the robot moves, electrical energy turns into kinetic energy, which is another name for movement energy.

3. The flashing lights show that electrical energy has been changed into light energy.

4. The robot makes a noise as it moves. Electrical energy has been turned into sound energy.

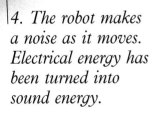

5. The robot gets warm. Movement energy has changed into heat energy.

Running Out of Energy

Most machines need energy to work. The energy from oil, coal, and gas is in danger of running out completely. Once these fuels, called fossil fuels, have been used up, there will be no way of replacing them.

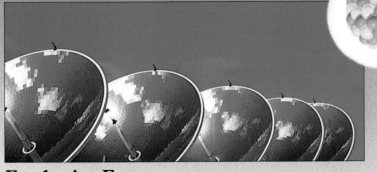

Everlasting Energy

The Sun's rays beat down on these solar panels. Heat is stored and used to make electricity. Energy from the wind and waves also provides power. Scientists are trying to find cheaper ways of capturing the endless supply of natural energy.

Splitting the Atom

Neutrons are tiny particles inside an atom. If a uranium atom takes in one extra neutron, it splits in half, releasing a huge amount of energy. Nuclear energy produces radioactive waste, which has to be handled and got rid of very carefully.

HEAT

The Sun's rays can make you very hot. The way heat rays move through air is called radiation. You feel warm because the radiation makes the molecules in your skin move about faster than usual. Heat comes from molecules moving around. It moves through solids by conduction – the molecules in a solid vibrate, bumping the heat along. Heat travels through air and liquids in a circular movement, called convection.

Heat moves along the wooden spoon by conduction. The spoon takes a long time to get hot because wood is not a good conductor of heat.

Snug as a Bug?

Heat doesn't travel easily through air, so materials that trap air keep you warm. This polar explorer is wearing clothes made of materials that insulate his body. This means they keep his body heat close to his body, where he needs it.

Tricky Fingers

If you dip one finger in hot water and another in cold, the hot water will feel hot and the cold water will feel cold. If you then dip both fingers in lukewarm water, your "hot" finger is tricked into finding the water cold, and your "cold" finger finds the water hot.

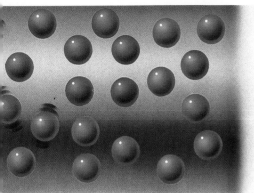

Good Conductors

If you heat a solid, its molecules jostle about, passing the heat from molecule to molecule. Just as a whisper moves along a line of children, so the moving molecules pass, or conduct, the heat from one end of the solid to the other.

Building Bridges

When most solids are heated, they get bigger, or expand. This is because the heat speeds up the molecules, and they get farther and farther apart as they move. Bridges are built with small gaps between the long pieces of metal, so there is room for the metal to expand on a hot day.

As the water reaches its boiling point, it evaporates into steam.

When the water near the heat source gets hot, it rises up toward the surface.

The cooler water near the surface will sink to the bottom of the pan, where it is then warmed up by the heat source.

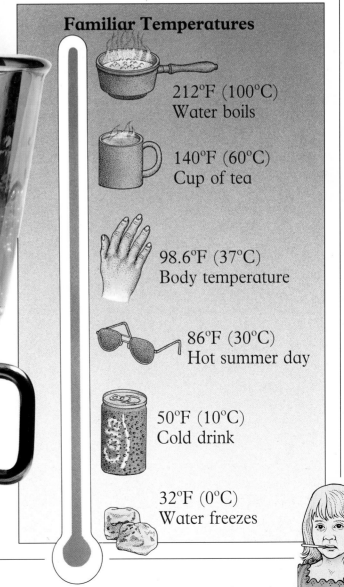

Familiar Temperatures

212°F (100°C)
Water boils

140°F (60°C)
Cup of tea

98.6°F (37°C)
Body temperature

86°F (30°C)
Hot summer day

50°F (10°C)
Cold drink

32°F (0°C)
Water freezes

The flames are a direct source of heat.

Metal is a good conductor of heat.

LIGHT

You may need to wear sunglasses on a sunny day because the bright light hurts your eyes. It is dangerous to look straight at the Sun. The Sun's light is not just blinding, it also travels to us very fast. In one second, light travels about 186,280 miles (300,000 km). If a straight beam of light has to pass through obstacles like convex and concave lenses, it changes direction. This is called refraction.

Hot Stuff
Most light comes from hot objects. A very hot object makes a very bright light. The Sun is white hot, and sunlight is the brightest natural light that we have.

Concave lenses curve inward in the middle.

This beam of light comes from a flashlight. A flashlight is a human-made light source.

Light bends outward when it passes through a concave lens.

Convex lenses bulge in the middle.

Retina

Pupil

Lens

Optic nerve

How We See Light
Light enters your eye through your pupil. It passes through a lens, which focuses the object you are looking at onto the retina. Millions of tiny cells inside the retina turn this upside-down image into electrical messages. The optic nerve carries these messages to your brain, which "sees" the image the right way up.

Light for Life
Plants always grow toward the light, even if, like this plant, they have to grow around corners to reach it! Light is very important for life. Plants need light to grow, and we need to eat plants, or animals that eat plants, to stay alive.

The Big Bang

Light travels faster than sound. When fireworks explode high in the sky, you see the lights before you hear the big bang. Light reaches your eyes more quickly than sound reaches your ears.

Over the Rainbow

Drops of rain act like tiny prisms. When light passes through raindrops, the colors of light are split up to form a rainbow.

When a beam of light passes through a prism, the colors split apart because each wavelength is bent a different amount.

Light travels in tiny waves. Light has a mixture of different wavelengths.

A prism is a solid, triangle-shaped piece of glass or plastic.

When light passes through a convex lens, it is bent, or refracted, inward.

When light is reflected, the beams of light bounce off the mirror at the same angle as they hit it.

When light hits an object that it can't travel through, like this mirror, a shadow forms behind the object where the light can't reach.

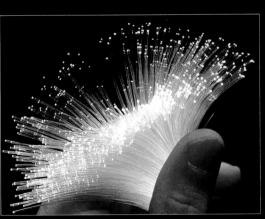

Busy Line

When you talk on the telephone, your voice is turned into laser light signals and sent down very thin fiberglass tubes called optical fibers. Up to 150,000 different conversations can be sent down just one of these optical fibers.

COLOR

Imagine waking up in a world without color. There would be no beautiful paintings or rainbows to look at and no bright shoes or clothes to wear. At night, when you switch off the light, all the bright colors around you suddenly disappear. This is because you cannot see the color of an object without light. White light can be split into all the colors of the rainbow – shades of red, orange, yellow, green, blue, indigo, and violet. When all these colors are mixed back together, they make white light again.

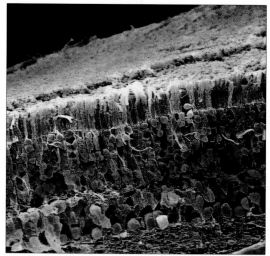

Color Cones
The inside of the back of your eye looks like this through a microscope. You have cells in the back of your eyes called cones, which send messages to your brain about the colors you see.

Seeing in Color
If you don't have all the different types of cones in your eyes, you may find it hard to tell some colors apart. A color-blind person may not be able to see the number on this color-blindness test.

White is the only color that can't be made by mixing the primary colors of paint together.

Seeing Red
We see things because light bounces off them. Light is actually a mixture of all the colors of the rainbow. When light hits these shoes, all the colors sink in, except the red color that is reflected back to your eyes.

Light Mixing
The colors of light behave differently from paint colors. When red, green, and blue light are mixed together, they make white light. The same colors of paint mix to make a dark color.

Paint Mixing

You can make new colors by mixing the primary colors of paint together.

Blue, yellow, and red are the primary colors of paint.

Red and yellow mix to make orange.

Blue and red mix to make purple.

Different shades can be made by adding more of one color than another.

Blue and yellow mix to make green.

Tasty Morsels

Which of these dinners would you like? Both meals would taste the same, but the food coloring in one turns you off before you start. Color can change our feelings about things, especially food.

Warning Colors

Colors are often used as a warning. This moth is poisonous, and its bright wings warn hungry birds to leave it alone. We also use colors to warn us of danger. A red traffic light tells us to stop, but a green traffic light means that it is safe to go.

SOUND

Astronauts talk to each other by radio because their voices can't travel through empty space. Sound travels in waves. When these waves move through air, the air molecules move quickly, or vibrate. If there are no air molecules, no sound is made, because there is nothing to vibrate. When you shout, the vocal cords in your throat vibrate. These vibrations pass through your mouth into the air, making the air itself vibrate. Your ear picks up the vibrations, and you can hear them as sound.

Deafening Decibels
The loudness of sounds is measured in decibels. When airplanes land, they reach a very high number of decibels. This ground controller is wearing ear protectors to keep from being deafened by the noise.

The bottle tops clink together when the jingling stick is shaken.

Lentils inside the shaker make a soft, rattling sound.

Strings vibrate as the instrument is plucked. The tighter the string, the higher the note.

Wailing Whales
Whales communicate underwater over huge distances. The sound of a big whale may travel hundreds of miles underwater. Sound travels faster and farther through liquids and solids than through air. This is because molecules in liquids and solids are more tightly packed.

Seeing Sounds
You can show that sound vibrations exist by hitting a tray next to a drum sprinkled with rice. The rice bounces up and down with the vibrations that the sound makes.

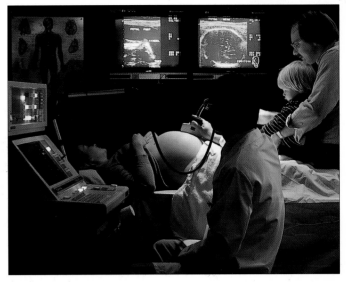

Bouncing Sound
This pregnant woman can see her baby before it is born. High-frequency sound waves are reflected as they reach the baby, making an image on the computer screen.

Hitting a metal plate makes it vibrate. You hear a loud and crashing noise.

What Is Frequency?
The number of complete sound waves that pass by in a second gives us the "frequency" of a sound. Frequency is measured in hertz. High notes have a high frequency. They make lots of vibrations and have a high number of hertz. Low notes have a low frequency.

Hearing Sounds
We cannot hear sounds of very high or low frequencies, but many animals can. It is impossible for us to hear these sounds because they are outside our hearing range.

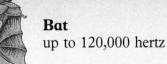

Bat
up to 120,000 hertz

Mouse
up to 100,000 hertz

Dog
up to 35,000 hertz

Cat
up to 25,000 hertz

Young person
up to 20,000 hertz

When a wind instrument is played, the air inside the tube vibrates to make a sound.

Blowing into the pipe makes the air inside it vibrate all the way along to the funnel at the end.

FORCE AND MOVEMENT

A rocket can only take off because a blast of energy forces it to move. Things move if they are pushed or pulled, or if they are high up to start with. The movement they make has a speed in a particular direction. How quickly they speed up depends on how big the force is and how heavy the moving thing is. Some forces make things move, but others stop things from moving. Friction is the name for the force that stops movement.

Push it!

Pull it!

Playing with Force
Forces can act in lots of different directions to change the shape of something. Try this for yourself with a lump of modeling clay.

Squeeze it!

Roll Apart
If one girl pushes the other, both will start to roll away from each other. When a force pushes one way, it also pushes equally in the opposite direction.

The go-cart wheels will keep moving until something stops them or slows them down.

If the passenger is heavy, it is hard to push the go-cart along and make it speed up.

Friction is a force that slows things down. The go-cart wheels rub against the ground, making friction.

Speed and Velocity

The time something takes to move a certain distance is called speed. Velocity is speed in a particular direction. A rocket's velocity is much greater than a snail's!

A snail moves at about 0.003 m/h (0.005 km/h).

A fast sprinter runs at about 22 m/h (36 km/h).

A race car reaches speeds of up to 210 m/h (338 km/h).

A rocket leaves the Earth's atmosphere at 25,000 m/h (40,000 km/h).

Down to Earth

When you jump, a strong force called gravity pulls you back down to Earth. Earth's gravity gets weaker as you travel away from it. On the Moon, gravity is much less strong, so astronauts can jump high with heavy packs on their backs before gravity pulls them back down again.

Pushing is a kind of force. The harder the boy pushes, the bigger the force on the go-cart.

Quick Stop

Without friction between its wheels and the ground, this truck could not move anywhere at all. The thick patterns on the tires, called tread, help the truck get a grip on the ground.

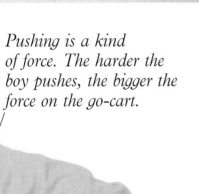

Good Performance

At high speeds, air rushes over the top of a race car, pushing it down onto the track. This makes the wide tires grip the track better, so the car can take turns faster than an ordinary car.

More pushing power is needed to start the go-cart than to keep it moving.

MACHINES

When you do a difficult sum, you are working hard, but this is not what scientists call work! In science, work is only done when something is moved – for example, lifted or turned around. Machines make it easier to move things, so less effort is needed to do a job. Bicycles help us move quickly. Like most machines, bicycles are made up of a number of small, simple machines. Wheels, axles, pulleys, gears, levers, slopes, and screws are all common simple machines.

Forced Apart

Wedges are simple machines that split things open. When a force hammers a wedge into a block of wood, the wood is pushed apart. A wedge is a kind of slope.

Saddle Sore?

It is possible to ride a long way on a bike – between 1922 and 1973 a Scottish man, Tommy Chambers, cycled 799,405 miles (1,286,517 km)!

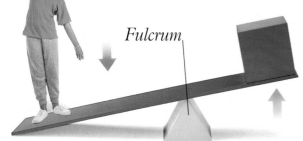

Fulcrum

Easy Does It

Levers make hard jobs easier. A seesaw is a kind of lever. The balancing point is called a fulcrum. The girl's weight is the force, and the box is the load.

Cables link the brake levers to the brake pads. Pulling the brake levers makes the brake pads stop the moving wheels.

Brake pads press against the wheel. They use friction to stop it from moving.

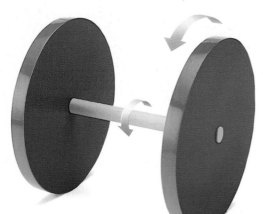

Wheel Genius

The wheel is one of our most important machines. Two wheels can be joined together by a pole, called an axle. A small movement of an axle makes a big turn of a wheel.

The wheel spins, or rotates, around an axle.

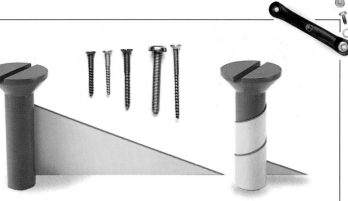

Difficult   Easy

Get into Gear
A toothed wheel that turns another toothed wheel is called a gear. Gears change the speed or direction of the moving part of a machine. The small wheel spins around twice as fast as the big wheel, turning in the opposite direction.

Uphill Climb
Slopes are simple machines. They make it easier to move things onto a higher or lower level. A screw is a kind of slope. If you could unwind the spiral grooves on a screw, they would flatten out as a slope.

A chain links the gears and the pedals to the back wheel. A small movement of the pedals is turned into a bigger turn of the wheel.

The chain is part of a pulley system.

Pedal power is the force that gets you started.

Light as a Feather?
Lifting up a weight with your bare hands is hard work. It is much easier to lift a weight by pulling down on the ropes of a pulley. If you double the number of pulley wheels, the same amount of effort will lift twice as many weights.

ELECTRICITY

We use electricity for heat, light, and machine power. The electricity we use is called current electricity. It flows along wires and cables and is so powerful that it is dangerous. Electricity is made when very tiny particles, called electrons, are forced to move. Turning on a light switch makes electrons bump into each other. This pushes an electric current along a wire, which lights up a bulb.

Electrons on the Move
If you flick one end of a line of marbles, they move along by knocking into each other. Electrons move along a wire in this way, making an electric current flow.

Lemon Battery
Stick a paper clip and a metal tack in a lemon. Your tongue connects them both to make an electric circuit. The tingling feeling you get is a small electric current!

1. Electricity flows out of the battery's negative terminal. The battery is a safe source of electricity.

2. The flow of electricity is called a current.

Static Magic
When electrons flow, they make current electricity. Static electricity is made when electrons just move from one place to another. Lightning is an example of when static electricity is released in nature. If you rub a balloon against your T-shirt, static electricity makes the balloon stick to you.

Good Conductors
Materials that let electricity pass through them are called conductors. These things are all good conductors of electricity.

5. The electric current flows back into the battery through the positive terminal.

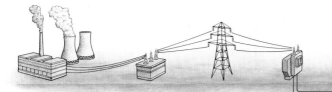

Power to the People
Electricity from power stations is sent along cables to transformers, which boost the power. Pylons hold the cables above the ground. Transformers then reduce the power so that the electricity is safe for us to use in our homes.

In the City
At night, it is easy to see how much people depend on electricity.

Go with the Flow
The battery, wires, bulb, and conductor all join up so the electricity can flow around. This is called a circuit.

3. This screw is being tested to see if it lets electricity pass through it.

4. The light bulb lights up when electricity is flowing through the circuit.

Warning!
Electricity can be dangerous – do not use electrical appliances without asking a grown-up first.

Good Insulators
Different materials can be tested to see if they let electricity pass through them. Some materials, like wood, plastic, cotton, and wax, do not conduct electricity. They are called insulators.

Shining Bright
A light bulb shines more brightly if a bigger current of electricity is allowed to flow through it. The tiny glowing wire inside the bulb is called the filament.

MAGNETS

Magnets are pieces of special material that have an invisible force that can push things away or pull things toward them. The biggest magnet of all is the world itself. Scientists think that as the Earth turns around, electricity is made in the hot metal deep down in the center. This electricity gives the Earth magnetic power. The Earth has two magnetic poles, called the magnetic North and South poles. Compass needles always point to the magnetic North Pole.

Magnetic Fields

A magnetic field is where a magnet has its power. If iron filings are sprinkled around a magnet, they gather together where the magnetic field is strongest. Two identical poles push each other away, so iron filings curve outward.
Two different poles attract. The iron filings run straight between them.

Left Out

Magnets only attract some kinds of material. Not all metals are attracted by magnets.

Magnets are fun to play with! These magnets are called horseshoe magnets because of their curved shape.

The area where the magnet has its power is called the magnetic field.

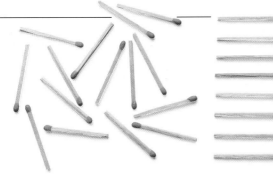

What Are Magnets?

Scientists think that atoms behave like tiny magnets. In a nonmagnetic material, the atoms face in different directions. In a magnet, all the atoms face the same way. Magnets lose their strength if they are hit, dropped, or heated, as this makes the atoms face in different directions.

The ends of a magnet are called its poles.

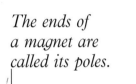

It is hard to push two identical poles together. The magnetic forces are pushing them apart.

Every magnet has two poles: a positive pole (+) and a negative pole (-).

It isn't easy to pull two different poles apart. The magnetic forces between them hold them close together.

Make a Magnet

If you stroke a needle about 50 times with a magnet, it will become magnetic. Stroking the needle in the same direction turns its atoms to face the same way.

Simple Compass

Compasses are made with magnets – see for yourself! Tape your magnetic needle to a piece of cork and float the cork in some water. It points the same way as a real compass needle – toward the magnetic North Pole.

Electricity and Magnets

Electricity is used to make magnets that can be switched on and off. This electromagnet is used to sort scrap metal. You can make an electromagnet by winding some wire around a nail and connecting it to a battery. The nail becomes magnetic.

WATER

Water can be fun, but it is also very important for life. It keeps our bodies working and also keeps every living thing on Earth alive. When water turns into a gas in the atmosphere, it is called water vapor. The air is made up of many different gases, and water vapor usually only makes up a tiny amount of the air. But without any water vapor in the air, we would have no rain or snow – in fact, we would not have any weather at all.

Thirsty?

Nothing can live without water. You couldn't survive more than a few days without it! More than two-thirds of your body is made up of water.

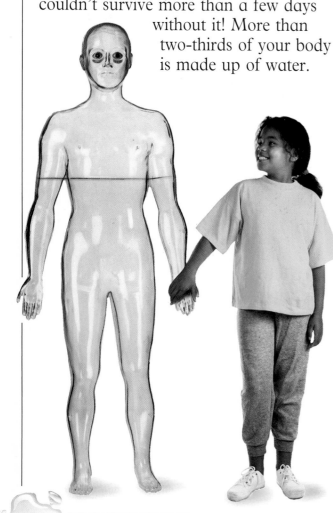

The salty seas contain 97 percent of the world's water.

Leaves on plants give off water vapor into the air.

The Sun warms water on land and at sea until it turns into water vapor. This is called evaporation.

Clouds are made when water vapor condenses on tiny specks of dust in the air.

Clouds get bigger as more water vapor condenses.

Rain falls when the water drops get too heavy to stay up in the cloud.

Water Cycle

The water we drink is recycled. This snow globe shows how water is always on the move.

Floating and Sinking

If you drop an apple, a force called gravity pulls it toward the ground. In water, apples do not sink because an upward force made on them by the water balances the force of gravity. Things float if they are less dense than water. Apples are less dense than water, so they float.

Big clouds can hold thousands of gallons of water.

Spilling Out

If you fill a glass of water to the brim, then drop in a toy truck, some water is pushed out, or displaced, from the glass. The amount of space something takes up is called its volume. The volume of displaced water is the same as the volume of the truck.

We drink fresh water. Only 3 percent of the world's water is fresh water, found in ice, lakes, and rivers, underground, and in the air.

Rain falls back into the rivers, lakes, and sea.

All Steamed Up

Your glasses steam up when you walk into a warm room from the cold. Hot air cools down on the cold glasses and forms tiny water droplets. This is called condensation.

Water from rivers and lakes flows into the sea.

WEATHER

It is difficult to escape from the weather! People are always interested in how, why, and when the weather is going to change. The study of weather is called meteorology. Meteorologists are scientists who find out about weather. It is only possible for meteorologists to tell what the weather will be like tomorrow if they know exactly what the weather is like today. This is why they have invented some very accurate ways of measuring the weather.

View from Space
Satellites give pictures of the weather all over the world.

Up in the Air
Balloons and special airplanes record weather information and send it back to ground level.

All at Sea
At sea, weather buoys measure air pressure and temperature.

This is an anemometer. It measures the speed of the wind.

Action Stations
Meteorologists collect measurements from all these instruments and send the information to weather forecasters.

Barometers record air pressure, which is the weight of air pressing down on the Earth's surface.

Thermometers tell us how hot or cold it is.

Wind vanes show the direction the wind is blowing from.

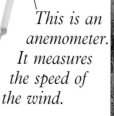

Rain gauges measure the amount of rain that falls.

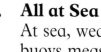

Weather Mountain

The mountain in the middle of this island affects the weather. Warm winds cool down and form rain clouds as they climb the mountain slopes. At the peak, the air is dry and cold, but as the air sinks on the other side of the mountain, it gets warmer again.

Warm winds from the northeast hit the north side of the island.

The mountain peak is snowcapped all year long because the air up there is always cold and dry.

The warm wind cools down as it climbs up the mountain. This makes rain clouds form.

The clouds disappear as they meet the warm air on this side of the mountain.

Weather Report

This television weather report shows what the weather is like all over the island. The symbols stand for different weather conditions.

Key

☀ Sunshine

⛅ Cloud

🌧 Rain

↙ Wind direction

The south side of the island is very hot and sunny.

MATERIALS

Sand

+

Limestone

+

Soda

=

The objects around you are made of different materials. The material that is used to make something is chosen for a particular reason. Some materials are very strong, so they are used to make tough things, like bike helmets. Others may be soft, so they can be used to make comfortable clothes, or cuddly things like teddy bears. Materials can be either natural or human-made. The ingredients of human-made materials are called raw materials.

Can You Tell?

It can be hard to tell whether something is natural or human-made. Human-made materials can be made to look and feel like natural materials. Human-made materials are made, or manufactured, from a mixture of natural raw materials.

Hard stone can be carved to make objects.

Glass bottle

This letter opener is made out of wood, a very common natural material.

Making Glass

The recipe for glass is very old. Sand, limestone, and soda are melted in an oven called a furnace. This makes molten glass, which can be used to make bottles.

Leather is a comfortable material made from animal skin. It is often used to make shoes.

Cotton is softer than wool. Its threads don't have as many sharp edges.

The Cutting Edge

Throughout history, new materials have been discovered that make a simple job, like cutting, easier.

The first cutting tools were made of rock.

Bronze was made by mixing together copper and tin.

Stainless steel cuts well and lasts a long time because it doesn't rust.

Clay Change
When materials are heated, chemical reactions happen. This means the materials change and take on new properties.

1. This lump of clay won't break if you drop it.

2. A potter has shaped the clay into a vase.

3. The heat of a kiln makes the vase lighter and drier. Drop it now, and it will smash to pieces.

4. A shiny glaze is baked onto the vase to make it waterproof, so it can hold water for flowers.

Plastics can be molded into different shapes, like this toy car.

Glass is waterproof and does not absorb smells or dirt. It is an ideal see-through container for drinks.

This corkscrew is made of a metal called steel. It is strong and can be easily shaped.

Plastic Revolution
The first plastic was made at the beginning of this century. Plastic is now a very common human-made material. Plastics are based on giant chains of molecules. Scientists call these molecules polymers. Oil and natural gas can be used as raw materials for plastic polymers.

Chain of molecules

Many clothes are made from human-made materials, such as this polyester shirt, which is strong and does not crease easily.

Paper is a human-made material. Wood is an important raw material of many kinds of paper.

BALANCE OF NATURE

We could not survive without food from animals or plants. Living things depend on other creatures or plants to stay alive. The order in which one group of living things eats another group of living things is called a food chain. If any one of the links in a food chain is taken out, the delicate balance is upset. Biologists study food chains and other aspects of the natural world. They also measure the effects of pollution on the environment.

If one kind of fish is caught faster than it can breed, the balance of the food web is upset.

Antarctic Food Web
A food web is made up of lots of food chains. The animals and plants in this food web are all found in the Antarctic Ocean near the South Pole.

Wither Away
Vegetables will always rot when they are thrown away. They are biodegradable and do not damage the environment. It is not easy to get rid of nonbiodegradable materials, because they do not rot. A lot of packaging is made of nonbiodegradable material. Some materials can be recycled and used again.

Blowing in the Wind

Wind carries pollution a very long way. In 1986, a nuclear accident at Chernobyl in Russia polluted countries as far away as Scotland, Sweden, and Italy.

1. An explosion at a nuclear power station sent up clouds of radioactive pollution.

2. In parts of Britain, rain fell from radioactive clouds. Farm animals ate the polluted grass.

3. Some cows' milk became radioactive and dangerous to drink for a while.

Killer whales eat Weddell seals and are the top predators in this food web.

Weddell seals dive deep to catch icefish and Antarctic cod.

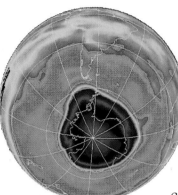

We Need Ozone!

About 12 miles (20 km) above Earth is a layer of ozone gas. Ozone stops the Sun's dangerous ultraviolet rays from harming us. Human-made chemicals called CFCs and halons make holes in the ozone layer, so ultraviolet rays can reach us more easily.

Icefish and Antarctic cod eat a large amount of animal plankton.

Animal plankton feed on plant plankton.

The Greenhouse Effect

The Earth is kept warm by a layer of natural gases that trap some of the Sun's heat. Pollution sends up more gases into this layer. Scientists think the Earth is getting warmer, because less and less of the Sun's heat can escape through this layer of pollution.

The food source at the bottom of this food web is plant plankton. These tiny water plants make their own food from the Sun.

TIME

You have a natural body clock that tells you when to fall asleep or wake up. Your body follows a circadian rhythm, which takes a whole day. Just like you, the Earth follows very regular patterns. It makes a complete turn every 24 hours, so that nighttime always follows the light of day. We measure the passing of time in years, months, days, hours, minutes, and seconds. People have found more and more accurate ways of measuring these units of time with different kinds of clocks.

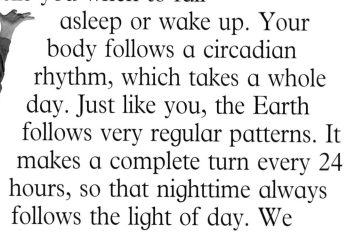

Day In, Day Out
Most living things have a regular rhythm of action and rest. Like many flowers, this crocus opens up by day and closes at night.

It gets dark when the Sun's light can't reach your side of the world and it falls into shadow.

Photo Finish
The time it takes to run a race must be measured very accurately. Seconds are divided up into very tiny parts, and one second is a long time in a race. The winner is often only a fraction of a second faster than the runner-up.

Moon Month
The Moon circles the Earth in a movement called an orbit. A lunar month is the time the Moon takes to make one orbit of the Earth.

What's the Time?
People used to tell the time by looking at sundials, water clocks, and sand timers. When pendulums were invented, clocks became more accurate. Today, time can be measured precisely by the vibrations of quartz in quartz clocks and atoms in atomic clocks.

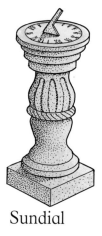

Sundial

The Turning World

The Earth never stops turning. It makes one full turn in 24 hours.

When the Sun's light hits your side of the world, it is daytime.

Time and Space

In just one second, light travels about 186,280 miles (300,000 km), so it goes an incredibly long way in a year. The distance light travels in a year is called a light-year. Enormous distances in space are measured in light-years.

One side of the world is always in darkness. This is called night.

The time of day is different in places that are far apart.

Slow Down

Albert Einstein, a scientist, said that a clock would slow down the closer it got to the speed of light. Years later, he was proved right. An atomic clock was flown around the world at a very fast speed. It slowed down by a millionth of a second during the flight.

Circling the Sun

The Earth moves around the Sun. A year is the time the Earth takes to make one orbit of the Sun.

Water clock

Sand timer

Pendulum clock

Quartz clock

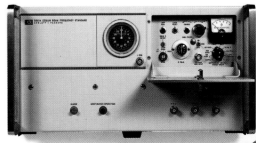

Atomic clock

SCIENCE IN OUR LIVES

3. *Communication satellites are stationed over the Atlantic, Pacific, and Indian oceans.*

Ideas from science can be used in a practical way to make inventions that help us in our lives. This is called technology. Technology is not a modern thing – the wheel was invented thousands of years ago and is still an important piece of technology. Inventions that solve problems are all around us. The computer is one of the most useful inventions of this century. Computer technology controls many kinds of machines, from the calculator in your hand to the satellites in orbit around the Earth.

2. *A transmitter dish sends the pictures to a satellite.*

1. *A television camera records an event on the other side of the world.*

Getting Smaller
Advances in technology lead to the design of smaller things. The first valve radios were very big. Smaller radios arrived when tiny transistors were invented. Today, radios as thin as credit cards are made, thanks to microchip technology.

1930s valve radio

Computer Car
In the future, computer screens may give car drivers useful information. Getting lost could become a thing of the past, if computers helped the driver decide which route to take.

1950s early transistor radio

1970s transistor radio

Transistors

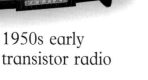

Modern radio

4. A satellite dish receives the pictures, which are then transmitted to your television set.

Catching a Satellite
Technology can go wrong. These astronauts from the space shuttle *Endeavor* are rescuing the television satellite *Intelsat 6*. The satellite had gone into the wrong orbit and had to be captured and sent off on the right orbit.

5. You can watch the concert on television as it happens.

In the Bag
Many of the things we take for granted are clever inventions. Look inside your bag!

Acrylic bag

Zipper

Glasses

Felt-tip pens

Pocket calculator

Cassette

Personal stereo

Plastic comb

Live Action
Any event, anywhere in the world, can be seen "live" thousands of miles away with the help of television satellite technology.

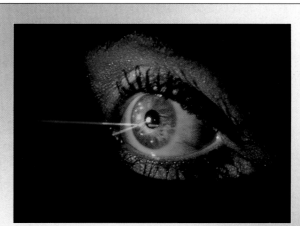

Lasers in Hospitals
Special lasers are used in hospitals. A laser can be beamed onto the eye for a split second. The tiny area that the laser hits gets very hot, making some difficult operations possible.

GLOSSARY

Air pressure The weight of air pressing down on the Earth's surface.

Atom The smallest amount of a pure substance that exists.

Biology The study of living things and the natural world.

Cell A living unit that makes up every living thing. Our bodies are made up of many billions of cells.

Chemical reaction A chemical reaction changes one or more different substances into a new substance.

Chemistry The study of what things are made of, how they behave, and how they can be mixed together.

Circuit Electricity flows from the power source in an unbroken loop. This loop is called the circuit.

Condensation When hot air cools down on a cold surface, tiny water droplets are formed. This is called condensation.

Conduction Heat travels through solids by conduction. Heat makes molecules in a solid vibrate, bumping the heat along.

Convection Heat travels through air and liquids in a circular movement called convection.

Crystal Crystals in solids are regular shapes, with faces that join at different angles.

Current The flow of electricity is called a current.

Decibel The loudness of sounds is measured in decibels.

Electricity Electricity is made when tiny particles, called electrons, are forced to move. Electricity we use is current electricity. Lightning is the release of static electricity in nature.

Energy Energy is needed for life and every movement in the universe. It is never made or destroyed but can change from one kind of energy into another.

Evaporation A liquid evaporates into a gas when molecules start to escape from its surface.

Expansion Solids, liquids, and gases get bigger when they are heated. This is called expansion.

Food chain The order in which one group of living things eats another.

Force A force can act in different directions to change the shape or position of an object.

Frequency Sounds travel in waves. The number of complete waves that pass by in a second gives the frequency of a sound.

Friction The name for the force that slows things down and stops movement.

Gas When a liquid is heated to its boiling point, it turns into a gas.

Gravity A strong force, called gravity, pulls objects back down to Earth. Gravity makes heavy and light objects fall to the ground at the same speed, if they are dropped from the same height.

Hertz Frequency of sound is measured in hertz.

Insulation Materials that stop the movement of heat or electricity are good insulators.

Laser A very intense beam of human-made light. Lasers can be directed onto a very small area or beamed across large distances.

Lens A curved piece of see-through material, like glass, that changes the direction of a beam of light.

Liquid A solid becomes a liquid when it gets hot enough to melt. A liquid flows more easily than a solid and can't form a rigid shape by itself.

Machine Machines make it easier to move an object, so less effort is needed to do a job.

Magnetism An invisible force that can attract or repel things. The area around a magnet where the magnet has its power is called the magnetic field.

Matter Everything is made up of matter. Matter can be a solid, a liquid, or a gas and can change from one of these states to another.

Molecule Molecules are made when different atoms join together.

Physics The study of how things in the universe work and behave.

Polymer Plastics are based on giant chains of molecules, called polymers.

Prism A solid, triangle-shaped piece of glass or plastic that splits a beam of light into the colors of the rainbow.

Property A special quality of a solid, a liquid, or a gas.

Radiation How heat rays travel through empty space.

Refraction The way that rays of light will bend as they pass from one material to another.

Solid A solid can keep its shape without needing a container to hold it. The molecules in solids are packed together tightly, in a regular way.

Technology A practical use of science. Ideas from science can be used to make technological inventions.

Velocity Speed in a particular direction is called velocity.

Viscous A thick liquid that doesn't flow very well is viscous.

Volume The amount of space taken up by a solid, a liquid, or a gas.

Wavelength The distance between two waves of light or sound.

INDEX

A

aerodynamics **6**
air **12, 17, 20, 26, 36, 38, 39**
air pressure **17, 38**
astronaut **26, 29, 47**
atom **12, 13, 19, 35**

B

bacteria **9, 10**
battery **19, 32, 33, 35**
biodegradable **42**
biology **6, 7**
botany **10**

C

cell **10, 11, 22, 24**
chemical reaction **7, 41**
chemistry **6, 7**
circuit **32, 33**
color **24**
color-blindness **24**
computer **46**
condensation **36**
conduction **20-21**
conductor **20, 32**
convection **20-21**
crystal **13**
current **32-33**

D

decibel **26**
density **37**
displacement **37**

E

Earth **17, 29, 34, 36, 38, 43, 44, 45, 46**
Einstein, Albert **45**
electricity **32-33, 34, 35**
electromagnet **35**
electrons **32**
energy **18-19, 28**
evaporation **21, 36**
expansion **21**

F

Fleming, Alexander **9**
food chain **42-43**
food source **43**
food web **42, 43**
force **6, 9, 28-29, 30, 31, 34, 35**
frequency **27**
friction **28, 29, 30**

G

gas **12, 15, 16-17, 36, 43**
gear **30, 31**
glass **23, 40, 41**
gravity **6, 9, 29, 37**
greenhouse effect **43**

H

heat **14, 16, 18, 20-21, 32, 43**
hertz **27**

I

insulation **20, 33**
invention **46, 47**

L

laser **23, 47**
lattice **13**
lens **22, 23**
lever **30**
light **22-23, 24, 32, 45**
light-year **45**
lightning **32**
liquid **12, 14-15, 16, 20**

M

machine **19, 30-31, 46**
magnetism **34-35**
matter **12**
meteorology **38**
molecule **12, 13, 14, 15, 16, 17, 20, 26, 41**
Moon **29, 44**

N

neutron **19**
nonbiodegradable **42**

O

optical fiber **23**
orbit **44, 45, 46, 47**
ozone **43**

P

physics **6, 7**
plankton **43**
plastic **23, 41**
pollution **6, 42, 43**
polymer **41**
prism **23**
property **12, 41**

R

radiation **20**
rainbow **23, 24**
reflection **23**
refraction **22**
reproduction **7, 10**

S

satellite **38, 46, 47**
solid **12-13, 14, 20**
sound waves **26, 27**
space **8, 26**
Sun **18, 20, 22, 36, 43, 44, 45**
surface tension **15**

T

technology **46, 47**
temperature **15, 21, 38**
time **29, 44-45**

U

ultraviolet rays **43**
universe **8, 18**

V

velocity **29**
vibrations **26, 27, 44**
volume **14, 37**

W

water **12, 15, 17, 36-37**
wavelength **23**

Z

zoology **10**

Acknowledgments

Photography: Michael Dunning, Steve Gorton, David Rudkin, James Stephenson.

Additional photography: Paul Bricknell, Jane Burton, Philip Gatward, David Johnson, Dave King, Stephen Oliver, Tim Ridley, Karl Shone, Clive Streeter, Kim Taylor, Andreas von Einsiedel, Jerry Young.

Illustrations: Roy Flooks, Mick Gillah, Tony Graham, Keith Hume, Pavel Kostal, Janos Marffy, Sean Milne, Colin Salmon, Rob Shone, Sonia Whillock, John Woodcock.

Models: Donks Models, Celia Allen.

Thanks to: Covent Garden Cycles; Tina Lewis; Ron Lobeck; mathematics and science equipment provided by NES Arnold Ltd, Nottingham, NG2 6HD; Meteorological Centre of Santa Cruz de Tenerife; National Wireless Museum, IOW; Rosendale School, London; Scallywags Child Model Agency; The Colour Company; The Design Museum, London; United Glass Ltd., Alison Verity.

Picture Credits

Allsport: Yann Guichaoua/Agence Vandystadt 18t, Pascal Rondeau 29b; **Bruce Coleman Ltd.:** Eric Crichton 16l; **The Colour Museum, Bradford:** 4, 25; **Garden Picture Library:** John Glover 44tl, J. S. Sira 44tr; **Hulton Deutsch Collection:** 45; **Image Bank:** Jacques Cartier 21, Douglas J. Fisher 26tr, Jeffrey M. Spielman 25b; Chris Alan Wilton 32; **Images Colour Library:** 7, 18b, 36; **Michelin:** 29c; **NASA:** 29t, 47t; **Natural History Museum, London:** 11; **NHPA:** Henry Ansloos 17; **Oxford Scientific Films:** Dean Lee 26b; **Photographers Library:** endpapers; **Redferns:** Mick Hutson 47c; **Science Photo Library:** Dr Jeremy Burgess 1, 13, CNRI 9tl, George Haling 46, Adam Hart-Davis 24b, Prof. P. Motta, Dept. of Anatomy, University 'La Sapienza', Rome 24t, NASA 26tl, 28, 43, David Parker 33, 38, St. Mary's Hospital Medical School 9tc & b, Alexander Tsiaras 27, 47b; **Sporting Pictures UK:** 44b; **Standard Fireworks:** 23tl; **Steel Can Recycling Information Bureau:** 35; **Tony Stone Worldwide:** 19b, Ken Biggs 19t, Arnulf Husmo 18c, Matt Lambert 3, 8, **ZEFA:** 9tr, 16r, 20t, & b, Thomas Dimock 13b, J. Feingersh 4, 23, R. Halin 15, NASA 22, Schroeter 23tr; **University of Bristol:** Dr. Mervyn Miles 13t.

t – **top**   l – **left**   tc – **top center**
b – **bottom**   c – **center**   tl – **top left**   tr – **top right**